GW00658062

Twisted Whiskers™ Fabulous Friends!

Twisted Whiskers™
Fabulous Friends!

RUNNING PRESS
PHILADELPHIA • LONDON

Library of Congress Control Number: 20055930823

ISBN-13: 978-0-7624-2513-6
ISBN-10: 0-7624-2513-X

This book may be ordered by mail from the publisher.
Please include $1.00 for postage and handling.
But try your bookstore first!

Running Press Book Publishers
2300 Chestnut Street, Suite 200
Philadelphia, PA 19103-4371

Visit us on the web!
www.runningpress.com

INTRODUCTION

friendship . . . what's life without it? Friends laugh together, cry together, do crazy things together—and are decidedly fabulous together! One of the strongest and most unbreakable bonds in existence, friendship improves the quality of our lives and raises our spiritual standard of living. When we're with true friends, we don't have to dress up, or put out the guest towels, or even finish our sentences—friends know us better than that.

This little volume illustrates through its quirky collection of outrageously fun photographs that

no matter what size, shape, color—or breed!—
friends are, true friendship is unconditional.
These cuddly characters are accompanied by
 simple wisdom that celebrates all
the good, the bad—and the
twisted—that make friendships
truly unique. Often strange but always inspira-
tional, TWISTED WHISKERS™ FABULOUS FRIENDS! is an
amusing tribute to the profoundly special bond
between friends.

We go together
perfectly.

I only look interested.

Throw me a
bone and give
me a hug!

You blow me away.

15

Your secret is
safe with me.

You give me
happy feet!

Opposites do attract.

I'd be lost
without you.

23

Is it my fault
your life isn't as
exciting as mine?

True friends can
deflate big heads
like no one else.

Two of a kind.

I'm always
here for you.

Need a girl talk?

You're a top dog!

You always help
me spring back
to my old self.

The thought of
you leaving has
put a knot in
my throat.

39

Stressed much?

Give me some paw!

43

Is something wrong?

Have the courage
to be yourself.

You're purrrfect.

There's nothing
to fear when a
friend is near.

You scratch my back,
I'll scratch yours.

Bad hair day?

You make me crazy!

Smell ya later!

Let's go dancing!

Chin up!

63

Staring contest . . .
ready . . . go!

Lean on me.

Do you need a
paw to hold?

You give me that warm, fuzzy feeling.

I'd never turn
my back on you.

*Let's go out
on the town!*

76

I'm proud to
be your friend.

You make me
feel ten feet tall.

You are head
and shoulders
above the pack.

Did somebody
say weekend?!

Count me in!
Where are we going?

Let's shake things up!

Want to come
out and play?

I'm hoppin we're
friends forever.

Where have you
been all my life?

Remember, I know where
your paws have been.

It's not easy being
a diva. (But, I manage.)

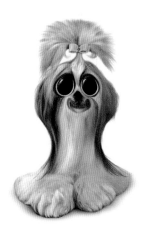

Ready for gossip.

I would bend over
backwards for you.

Is it me or is
everyone else crazy?

Dogs are from Mars,
cats are from Venus.

106

Do you want to
talk about it?

Who says we
are too old to monkey
around together?

Smile if you're
a cat lover!

We have a
twisted relationship. . .

butt I love you anyway!

Like a licking?

Something on
your mind?

Why the long face?

You bring sunshine
to my life.

I'm not drunk.
I'm always like this.

125

Girl, you are hot stuff!

This book has been bound
using handcraft methods and
Smyth-sewn to ensure durability.

The dust jacket and interior were
designed by Matt Goodman.

The text was
edited by Jennifer Leczkowski.

The text was set in
Spunky Jes and
Barnyard Gothic.